About Fish

About Fish

A Guide for Children

Cathryn Sill

Illustrated by John Sill

Ω

PEACHTREE

ATLANTA

For the One who created fish.

—*Genesis* 1:1

Published by
PEACHTREE PUBLISHERS, LTD.
1700 Chattahoochee Avenue
Atlanta, Georgia 30318-2112
www.peachtree-online.com

Text © 2002 Cathryn P. Sill
Jacket and interior illustrations © 2002 John C. Sill

Illustrations painted in watercolor on archival quality 100% rag watercolor paper
Text and titles typeset in Novarese from Adobe Systems

Manufactured in Singapore

10 9 8 7 6 5 4 3 2 1
First Edition

ISBN 1-56145-256-4

Library of Congress Cataloging-in-Publication Data

Sill, Cathryn P., 1953–
    About fish : a guide for children / written by Cathryn Sill ; illustrated by John
Sill.-- 1st ed.
            p. cm.
Summary: Introduces various species of fish, describing their food needs, body
structures, protective mechanisms, habitats, and reproduction.
        ISBN 1-56145-256-4
    1. Fishes--Juvenile literature. [1. Fishes.] I. Sill, John, II. Title.
    QL617.2 .S56 2002
    597--dc21   2001005568

About Fish

Fish live in water.

They may be found in nearly freezing water...

PLATE 2
Arctic Char

or in warm tropical water.

Fins help fish swim.

PLATE 4
Rainbow Darter

They can breathe underwater because they have gills.

PLATE 5
Bluegill

Fish protect themselves in many ways.

PLATE 6
Porcupine Fish

Most have tough skin covered by scales.

PLATE 7
Longnose Gar

The skin of a fish is slippery.

PLATE 8
Chinook Salmon

Fish may be colored to look like their surroundings…

PLATE 9
Pacific Halibut

or marked in other ways that fool their enemies.

PLATE 10
Foureye Butterfly Fish

Many fish live together in groups called schools.

Plate 11
Lookdown

Some baby fish are born alive, while others hatch from eggs laid by the mother.

Most fish eat meat.

PLATE 13
Largemouth Bass

Fish keep growing as long as they live.

PLATE 14
Whale Shark

It is important to protect fish and the places where they live.

Afterword

PLATE 1
Fish* live in almost all fresh and salt waters of the world. Most live in a specific habitat, and only a few species move between oceans and rivers. The Brown Trout, a freshwater native of Europe, was introduced to North America in 1883.

PLATE 2
The colder waters of the world have fewer fish species than tropical (warm temperatures year-round) or temperate (warm temperatures during some months of the year and cold during other months) waters. Arctic Char live in the cold waters of the north. Char that live in fresh water are more brightly colored than those living in the ocean. Arctic Char are an important source of food for people and animals in cold northern areas.

PLATE 3
Fish that live in warm tropical waters are generally more brightly colored than those that live in cooler waters. Brilliant colors and bold patterns may help them blend in with the light and shadows of their environment. The vividly colored Queen Angelfish is hard to see against the colorful coral reefs in its habitat.

PLATE 4
Fins help fish move through the water. They use them to steer, balance, and stop. Rainbow Darters are little fish (up to 3 inches long) that live near rapids in clear streams. They are called darters because they "dart about" using their tail and pectoral fins. Rainbow Darters are easily harmed by pollution, mud, and silt.

*Note: Scientific guides generally use the plural form "fishes" when referring to a number of different species. For the sake of simplicity, we have chosen to use the plural form "fish."

PLATE 5

A fish has gills instead of lungs. It gulps water through its mouth. The water flows over its gills, which take oxygen from the water. The water then goes out through openings on the sides of the fish's head. The Bluegill is one of the most popular freshwater game fish in the United States. Bluegills thrive in farm ponds and lakes.

PLATE 6

All but the largest fish are in danger of being eaten by predators. The Porcupinefish protects itself by swallowing water or air and inflating its body like a balloon. Its raised spines and puffed-up body make a prickly mouthful that is hard for other fish and animals to swallow.

PLATE 7

Most fish have a protective covering of scales. Fish are born with all the scales they will ever have. Some species of fish have scales that are smooth and flat. Others have scales that are rough like tiny teeth. The heavy, diamond-shaped scales of the Longnose Gar offer so much protection that these fish have few enemies.

PLATE 8

The slimy substance produced by special glands in the skin helps fish move easily through the water. This mucus also protects fish from infections. Salmon migrate from the ocean to rivers to spawn or lay their eggs. The Chinook (or King) Salmon is the largest type of salmon. It grows up to 4 feet long and may weigh 100 pounds.

PLATE 9

Flatfish swim on their sides along the ocean floor. The fish in this group are not born flat. As they grow, their bodies change shape and their eyes move to one side of their heads. Flatfish are colored in ways that blend in with their environment. The Pacific Halibut is a valuable commercial fish that grows to nearly 9 feet in length and weighs up to 800 pounds.

PLATE 10

Some fish have markings that protect them from enemies. The black eye-spot on the rear of the Foureye Butterflyfish and the black stripe through its eye confuse predators. It is hard to tell which end is the head; enemies don't know if this fish is coming or going.

PLATE 11

Fish travel in schools to take advantage of "safety in numbers." Schooling may also make it easier for the fish to find food and mates. Lookdowns are hard to see head-on because their bodies are very thin and flat. When you look at them from the side, you can see the silvery iridescence on their skin.

PLATE 12

Like all seahorses, female Lined Seahorses lay their eggs in a special pouch on the male's belly. He carries the eggs in this brood pouch until they hatch and pop out. The male Threespine Stickleback makes a nest from vegetation for the 77 to 190 eggs the female lays. He guards the eggs until they hatch and stays with the young until they can care for themselves. Not all fish guard their eggs and young.

PLATE 13

Many fish eat other fish. They also eat worms, insects, shellfish, and other water animals. A few eat water plants. The Largemouth Bass eats other fish, crayfish, insects, frogs, and even sometimes a baby duck. Many people enjoy fishing for Largemouth Bass.

PLATE 14

As a fish grows, its scales grow with it. It is sometimes possible to tell the age of a fish by counting the growth rings on its scales. Whale Sharks, the largest fish in the world, may grow up to 60 feet in length. They eat tiny shrimp and fish that they strain from the ocean. Whale Sharks are harmless to people.

PLATE 15

Fish are enormously important. They provide food for other animals and for millions of humans. Many people earn their living through commercial fisheries or enjoy recreational fishing. Pollution from sewage and industrial waste, as well as silt caused by erosion, harm fish. We need to protect fish by keeping our waterways clean. The Yellowfin tuna is a valuable food fish and a prized game fish.

Cathryn Sill is an elementary school teacher in Franklin, North Carolina, and the author of ABOUT BIRDS, ABOUT MAMMALS, ABOUT REPTILES, ABOUT INSECTS, and ABOUT AMPHIBIANS. With her husband John and her brother-in-law Ben Sill, she coauthored the popular bird-guide parodies, A FIELD GUIDE TO LITTLE-KNOWN AND SELDOM-SEEN BIRDS OF NORTH AMERICA, ANOTHER FIELD GUIDE TO LITTLE-KNOWN AND SELDOM-SEEN BIRDS OF AMERICA, and BEYOND BIRDWATCHING, all from Peachtree Publishers.

John Sill is a prize-winning and widely published wildlife artist who illustrated ABOUT BIRDS, ABOUT MAMMALS, ABOUT REPTILES, ABOUT INSECTS, and ABOUT AMPHIBIANS and coauthored the FIELD GUIDES and BEYOND BIRDWATCHING. A native of North Carolina, he holds a B.S. in Wildlife Biology from North Carolina State University.